and th

Anya Smith and Peter Adamson

P&LA

First published 2025 by P&LA © Anya Smith (b. 2010) and Peter Adamson (b. 1946), 2025

ISBN 978-1-0369-1805-7

Designed and typeset by Charlie Webster,
Production Line, Minster Lovell, Oxford
Printed by Short Run Press, Exeter, UK

If anyone protested, the soldiers came calling
the dungeons were crowded, the conditions appalling,
but while everyone in Morvan was fearful and sad,
little Anya Castagna was burning-hot mad!

New King for Old

Once upon a time in a faraway land,
stood a crumbly old castle, more homely than grand,
a bit draughty and spidery, though comfortable enough
for the King and his family and a Dalmatian called Ruff.

The land was called Morvan and so was the King
who had ruled many years with his Queen, Sue-Li Ling.
The people he ruled were called the Morvanis,
and had no need at all of weapons or armies.

For Morvan in those days was peaceful and rich,
without dragons or monsters and even the witch –
who lived in a cave at the back of beyond –
was kindly and wise, and really quite fond

of the Morvani children who came once a year
to pay their respects and drink ginger beer
(her name was Morwena and her age was unknown,
she could waggle her ears and play the trombone).

King Morvan was sprightly but well over ninety
and the people he governed – ever so benignly –
all feared for the time when his son took the crown
with his terrible temper and permanent frown.

Prince Trevelyan was sinister, moody and cold,
and interested only in soldiering and gold;
he followed his pleasure wherever it led
and ate puppies for breakfast, or so it was said.

On their phones one May morning, the Morvanis all read
that the King was unwell and had taken to bed.
By noon a great crowd had surrounded the palace
all fearing the King's life was now in the balance.

Inside the King's chamber, all was silent and dark,
for the light hurt his old eyes, which still had their spark,
and his courtiers were quiet when closing the doors
while old Ruff lay there whimpering, his nose on his paws.

Outside in the square, the crowd stared at the windows guessing which was the King's chamber and if those were the curtains that might soon be drawn
to show that King Morvan the Kind was no more.

Meanwhile, in a different part of the palace,
Crown Prince Trevelyan, all cheerful and callous,
was trying on the king's robes as well as his crown
and using two mirrors to practise his frown,

while out in the square there was pointing and muttering,
as over the palace a black flag was now fluttering.
And from thousands of throats there arose a great groan
for the curtains on the King's life had indeed now been drawn.

Soon two heralds stepped out on the rickety balcony
where the old King had liked to practise his falconry,
to sound a loud fanfare as Trevelyan appeared
to be crowned King of Morvan, just as they feared.

The new King frowned down and held up his sword
for them all to be quiet – they must hear every word –
and the people soon knew they were facing great trouble
when he said that from now on their taxes would double.

Now the Morvanis had always paid taxes to the King,
every Summer and Autumn and Winter and Spring,
and they'd grumbled a bit, but they'd known it was fair
to give some of their money, quite a large share,

to the King in his castle, it was one of the rules
and paid for the doctors and teachers and schools
and for bridges and roads and helping the poor,
and for constables and firefighters and very much more.

If all paid their taxes, there'd be no hunger or cold,
and all would be looked after when they grew old.
But Trevelyan, it seemed, had quite different ideas
as he raised both his arms, expecting their cheers

when he grandly announced something very alarming –
his intention to create a Morvani army
and to build a new palace fit for a King
with gold-plated balconies and all kinds of bling.

There followed a silence, then a voice from the crowd –
'We don't think it's right! It should not be allowed!'
But as soon as the words had left the man's lips
the King's men were after him with handcuffs and whips.

Soon he was caught and led screaming away
to the dungeons where the new king said he would stay.
'Now everybody go home!' he said with great malice,
'and never again come this close to the palace'.

Anya Castagna

Twelve months have now passed, a year of great miseries
for the Kingdom of Morvan and all the Morvanis.
No matter how hard they worked or which way they turned,
the King took three-quarters of all that they earned.

Their taxes, it seemed, were all spent on the war
(for Trevelyan had invaded the country next door).
No money was left for looking after the land
or helping anybody who needed a hand.

There were signs of the problem wherever you looked:
the doctors had no medicine, the schools had no books,
the hospitals were closed and the roads all had holes,
and instead of roast beef, the people ate moles.

One family there was who had not paid their tax
which wasn't a case of just being lax,
they'd chosen to spend the money instead
on good food and medicine for an aunt, sick in bed.

This, you should know, was the family Castagna -
a mum, and a dad, and a daughter called Anya.
Now Anya was eleven and quite tall for her age
with mid-length brown hair that shadowed the page

of the book she was reading in her bedroom that day
when the soldiers arrived to take her father away.
'You've not paid your taxes,' the sergeant-at-arms said,
and one of the soldiers put a gun to his head.

That night in her bed Anya wept 'til she slept
for the dad that she loved who was now being kept
in Trevelyan's dungeon with no light or fresh air
with flies in his gruel and spiders in his hair.

They wrote to the King but he never replied,
for Trevelyan, of course, had far too much pride
to bother with those who wrote tedious letters –
ignorant people, always bothering their betters.

Another month passed, and the suffering grew worse;
as if all the Morvanis were under a curse.
Perhaps, it was said, Queen Sue-Ling might help,
but no one, it seemed, now knew where she dwelt.

It was thought she'd been exiled, put into a nunnery,
where she had to say prayers and work in the scullery,
Meanwhile Trevelyan was enjoying the wealth
he stole from the people at the cost of their health.

If anyone protested, the soldiers came calling
the dungeons were crowded, the conditions appalling,
but while everyone in Morvan was fearful and sad,
little Anya Castagna was burning-hot mad!

Morwena's Cave

One Saturday morning, she had an idea
and crept out of the house so no one would hear,
and forgetting to take her gloves, hat or coat,
and forgetting to feed the pig and the goat,

and forgetting to remember to call at the florist
she set off at a trot on the path through the forest,
a-running and a-jumping over fence, stream and ditch,
to see if she could find ... Morwena the witch.

Her plan was to beg her for only one thing -
would she please, please, put a spell on the King
to make him release all the people from prison
and lower the taxes that had so steeply risen?

Now going on her own to the old witch's grotto
was something that frightened her really a lotto.
But Morwena was kind, so everyone said,
and would do her no harm (would she still be in bed?)

Anya half knew the way. They'd been only last year,
with a ton of cheese sandwiches and two crates of beer,
but they'd gone on the bus, the whole of the village,
with laughing and singing and quite a lot of spillage.

But now the path wasn't clear, the sunlight had gone,
And of signs and directions there were absolutely none.
The forest all around her was dense, wild and dark,
when always before it had seemed like a park.

But turn back she would not, she had to be brave,
she had to see Morwena, she had to find her cave.
She'd been running for miles, she'd been running for hours,
And she'd completely forgotten to buy any flowers.

So she stopped for a moment, her feet and her knees hurt,
and picked a few violets and daisies and sneezewort
and when she looked up there were cliffs all around,
and where there were cliffs a cave might be found!

And sure enough, now, as she peered through the trees,
she saw the witch's washing, a-blowing in the breeze,
long cloaks with wide sleeves hung up in a circle
newly washed and pegged out, all spotlessly purple.

Anya slowed to a trot, then a walk, then a creep.
It was still rather early. Would Morwena be asleep?
Oh dear, it might give her an unpleasant shock
to just suddenly appear, but there was nowhere to knock.

In a hesitant voice, she called out 'Hello - it's just me,'
but probably the witch couldn't hear her or see
that someone had come to pay her a visit.
But just then she heard someone calling 'Who is it?'

And then came a sound from deep in the cave,
it began with a murmur and grew like a wave,
a rushing and a bubbling and a rumbling sound
that grew louder and louder, quite shaking the ground,

and suddenly the witch was standing right there
in her long purple gown and her rats'-tails of hair,
her arms held so high that her sleeves filled the sky.
Anya's heart beat so hard and her mouth felt so dry.

But scared as she was of the old witch's powers,
she took a step forward and offered the flowers.
'Why, thank you,' said Morwena, 'that's really, like, thoughtful,
and wild ones are nicer than those that are boughtful.'

Then seeing her visitor was quite pale with fear
She gave a kind smile, though it looked a bit queer.
Anya wanted to explain but stuttered and stammered
and feared that Morwena would think her ill-mannered.

'Don't worry my dear, I can tell where your heart is,
are you hungry at all? I can give you some Smarties,'
said the witch as she launched the flowers to the stars
and when they came down they were in a glass vase.

Anya managed to thank her but still did not smile
it wasn't for tricks she'd come many a mile,
but for something important she wanted to plead for
and courage was what she now had a need for.

With a bow and a wave the witch invited her in
but from the mouth of the cave there came such a din,
a howling and a shrieking like a ghost in a spin,
that Anya began trembling all over again.

But once she had entered the hole in the rock
the strangest thing happened – another kind of shock -
for the noise could be heard only outside the cave
while inside in the gloom it was quiet as the grave.

'Do sit down,' said the witch, 'I'll make tea if I'm able,'
and the very next moment there was tea on the table.
Anya sat on a rock – it was soft as a sofa
while Morwena poured tea and looked her visitor over.

'Now tell me, my dear,' said the witch in a voice
that was gentle and kind as she offered the choice
of cream cheese with sprinkles or bread and black jam
'what is it that's made you come find where I am?

'I wasn't expecting anyone 'til the back end of June
and today is still May and, like, a long way too soon,
but a visit is nice when you live on your own
and spend all the day, like, looking at your phone.'

Anya sipped at her tea, exhausted from walking,
and wished that the witch would very soon stop talking.
Her mother had told her when someone lives alone,
if they get half a chance they go on and on.

'I shouldn't go on so,' Morwena eventually declared,
'but I thought it might help you, like, not to be scared?
Now please do tell me why you've come all this way
on your own through the forest so early in the day.'

Anya put the cup down and started to tell
how they'd loved the old king and all had been well
until he had died and Trevelyan was crowned
and taxed all the people to their very last pound

and kept all the money for himself and his friends
so all the Morvanis were at their wits' ends,
their houses all leaking, their clothes full of holes
and instead of pork sausages they were forced to eat moles.

And then, though she tried, she couldn't help it and cried
when she came to the part when the soldiers arrived
and her dad was marched off, locked up by Trevelyan –
'He might already be dead, he might even be a skeleton!'

The witch gave her a tissue from the box in her sleeve
and when Anya looked up she could clearly perceive
that a few tears had escaped from the witch's old eyes
and run down her face in the grooves and the lines.

'I was hoping,' said Anya, 'you might know of a spell
that could kill King Trevelyan and send him to Hell?'
Then the witch took her hand, and felt all her pain,
and shaking her head she began to explain

that killing the King was the wrong thing to do
as fighting hatred with hatred never would do.
'Believe me my dear, I'm a thousand years old,
and when people start killing it, like, gets out of control?'

'That's not the solution you wish for so much,
and besides,' she went on, 'the problem is such
that if Trevelyan were dead the crown would just pass,
to his cousin, Bozolopolos, who might well be worse.'

'The cool thing to do,' said Morwena at last
'is to, like, forget about the way it's been done in the past?
The cool way today to arrange all such things,
is for all of us guys to, like, choose our own kings?'

'Cool!' Anya said, 'like, a King with a heart?
My mum or my dad would be a good start.'
'But the thing with a king,' said the witch with a twitch,
is that, even with good ones, there's always a hitch.

When they die and then fly to the throne in the sky ...
... Oh dear, I thought I was getting the hang of this rhyme ...
Their son becomes king whether you like it or not,
And he might be a genius or he might be a clot.

Oh dear, thought Anya, bored near to paralysis,
I do wish she'd stop all this political analysis
and get to the point and brew up a potion
to get rid of Trevelyan without all this commotion.

Just then the old witch stood up from her rock
and Anya could see she wore only one sock
as she followed Morwena deep into the cave
past a tangle of wires and a vast microwave.

'Is this where you mix things and make up your potions?'
'No, no,' said the witch, 'such, like, old-fashioned notions?
I'm not into cauldrons or curses or spells,
or concoctions or lotions or potions or gels.

'I may be in need of advanced gerontology,
but I'm right up to date with the latest technology.
A thousand I may be, but I'm not yet doolally,
in fact I've been head-hunted by Silicon Valley.'

With this she sat down at an odd-looking keyboard
and began tipping and tapping until Anya grew e-bored,
while the moon-shaped screen showed letters and numbers
and curious symbols like stars and cucumbers.

And all of the time she was tapping and fumbling,
she was chuntering and muttering and cursing and grumbling:
'I wish people wouldn't do all this, like, spamming?
It gets in the way when a girl's, like, programming?'

Anya eventually stood up and looked all around her,
inspecting the cave 'til the witch came and found her.
In Morwena's hands now was a flat wooden box
tied up in a bow with one of her socks.

'Here you are my dear, I've made you a present,'
(there was even a gift card in the shape of a crescent).
'Are you any good with, like, computers and stuff?'
I myself, I confess, am, like, something of a buff?

'Anyway, don't scroll around on, like, TikTok and Amazon,
just switch on, hit the icon, and straightaway log on
to my very own website – worldwidewitches.com –
then enter the password – 'tiddlyompompompom' –

all one word, lower case, no hyphen or dash
and enter it carefully or the whole thing might crash.
I think that's the password,' the witch wondered aloud,
'Then click on the link that says 'Coven in the Cloud'.

'From there it's intuitive, like, easy to follow?
Though it's probably better to wait till tomollow
before you attempt to, like, connect to the Coven,
I'll message them first and tell them you're coming.'

Then Morwena took pity on her tired little visitor
and offered her breakfast of toadflakes and vinegar.
'Very kind, but I need to get home in a hurry
'cos Mum will already be starting to worry.'

'Come again,' said the witch, 'don't make it, like, annual.
And besides it's quite likely you'll be needing the manual.
I can see that you're tired, so off you go with your tablet,
but it's such a long way, should I call you a cablet?'

All the King's Icons

'Where have you been? It's really too bad.
I thought I'd lost you as well as your dad.'
'Don't worry,' said Anya, 'I've just been for a walk
and now, if you don't mind, I'm too tired to talk.'

That night, Anya yawned and went early to bed
to open the card and read what it said:
'Dear Anya, I do hope you'll use my gift wisely,
and for your little hands it will not be too sizely,

because if you are brave and patient and cunning
and don't fool about with, like, playing and funning,
you'll find ways to solve, like, all of your issues?
(After you'd gone, I needed a new box of tissues.)'

Then Anya untied the witch's smelly old sock
and opened the box, there wasn't a lock,
and inside she found – it quite made her blink –
the very latest iPad in her favourite pink!

The tablet had a posh screen and a button or two,
but how could it help? What could it do?
And then she remembered she had to log on
to Morwena's website, worldwidewitches.com.

It happened so fast, it was so unexpected,
as almost immediately the tablet connected
and Morwena appeared right there in her hand:
'This iPad, dear Anya, is your magic wand.

'You just need to visit the Worldwide Witches' Coven
(it sounds very grand, but there's only a dozen).
I'm going to be watching it all on my screen,
or one of them anyway, I've got, like, umpteen.

And if you should need me, as you're only a learner,
click the pointy black hat in the top left-hand cerner.'
Then Morwena waved goodbye but stayed on the screen
and picked up a copy of Witch Magazine.

Anya stared at the tablet, then turned down the sound
and nervously clicked on 'The Coven in the Cloud'.
Then up came a box that asked for her password
which she typed in carefully then suddenly heard

her mum's weary footsteps on the bare wooden stairs
as she came slowly to bed, full of worries and cares.
Anya fumbled and thumbled to turn the screen off
and covered up the beep with an unnecessary cough.

When all had gone quiet she dived under the duvet
(could she use her new iPad to also watch movies?)
Knees bent so the duvet rose up like a tent,
she turned down the brightness by fifty per cent.

And now at her fingertips were pictures and symbols
and some were like buttons and some were like thimbles.
One said 'King's palace' and another said 'King's table'.
There was one for his 'kennels' and another his 'stable'

and scrolling and tapping with a 'ping' and a 'ding'
she found dozens of icons to do with the King:
there was an app for his garden and one for his shed,
and one for his butter and one for his bread.

'I don't know what it means but it definitely seems
there's an icon for everything, even his dreams.'
More icons appeared as she swiped to the right –
it was the strangest thing ever in the middle of the night.

Next day Anya helped her Mum with the washing,
the frocks and the smocks and the socks all a-sloshing
around in the tub 'til everything was clean
(her Mum didn't have a washing machine).

But soon after seven, Anya yawned wide and said
'It's been a very long day, and I'm ready for bed.'
Her mum looked astonished because every other night
Anya didn't want to go to bed or turn out the light.

Teeth brushed, face washed, a prayer said for her dad,
she took out the iPad and climbed into bed,
then waited impatiently five minutes more
until all had gone silent and she really felt sure

she could power up the iPad and turn down the screen
and start to work out what on earth it could mean –
all those pictures and icons and folders and apps
and arrows and lights and symbols and maps.

But there was only one way to see what might happen
And that was to decide on one app to tap on.
But which should she choose? She had no idea,
and tapping on any of them filled her with fear.

But holding her breath, her face in a grimace,
she tapped on the symbol for Trevelyan's Palace
and immediately saw an astonishing scene
as the inside of the palace took over the screen.

Never had anyone beheld or ever been told,
of so much extravagance, so much silver and gold:
silk tapestries and curtains and precious antiques
and cages of budgies with what looked like gold beaks.

At the foot of the screen were more of the symbols
labelled 'Bedroom' and 'Kitchen' – it gave her goose pimples –
she could visit the whole palace, each chamber and room,
by scrolling and swiping and using the zoom.

She saw straightaway all was gold, yellow or red –
the King had picked them for everything, even the bed –
and nothing in the palace was what you would call
either blue, brown or green, really nothing at all.

Then Anya noticed, top right of the screen,
a rainbow of colour, from violet to green.
Taking a guess what this might be for
she pulled out the stylus and started to draw

and before very long she had learned to drag down
any colour in the rainbow, plus grey, black and brown.
Within a few minutes she had re-decorated
Several rooms of the palace in the colours the King hated!

By now she was tired and beginning to blink
for the screen hurt her eyes and she was starting to think
'What good will it do? I can't get rid of the King
or bring my dad back with just a ping and a ding.'

Next morning her mum said a very strange rumour
had put everyone in town in a very good humour,
and one of the King's servants had sworn it was true –
some rooms in the palace had turned brown, green and blue!

Apparently the King had flown into a rage
and shouted at his ministers and walloped a page.
He'd shaken so much he'd wobbled off his crown
and eventually been forced to go and lie down.

The Morvanis, it seemed, were all enjoying the tale –
'What's up, love?' said her mum, 'You're really quite pale.'
'Just a little bit tired,' said Anya, and thought that it might
probably be as well to have another early night.

After putting on her jim-jams and bolting her porridge
She crawled under the duvet and screwed up her courage
to tap on the icon marked 'Dungeon and Cellar'
though dreading to think about what it might tell her.

Would it show that her father was starving or dead?
Would his legs be in chains, all bloody and red?
She tapped next on the icon for the great dungeon door,
and the screen began flashing 'Are you sure? Are you sure?'

She clicked 'Yes' and opened the scary dark prison.
There were no windows or lights as she made herself listen
to the moans of the prisoners, trying to focus her eyes
on the silhouettes and scarecrows, some beginning to rise.

Whether one was her father there was no way to tell,
or to see any more in the gloom of that cell,
so she left-clicked on 'Home' and was left with her fears
and the contrasting brightness now shone in her tears.

The next night again she dived under the covers
and began to select icons, first one then others –
King's food and King's wardrobe, King's horses, King's dogs
King's music and e-mails, and all the King's blogs,

and for each there were menus and buttons and sliders –
for every little detail, even mouses and spiders.
Everything in the palace it seemed she could change,
there was nothing in the King's life she couldn't re-arrange.

She could change the behaviour of his dog and his cat
Just by pressing on this, or clicking on that.
She could put out the fires and make the palace go cold;
she could untie the King's shoes and hide all his gold;

she could turn on the taps and turn off the lights;
she could muzzle his dogs and disarm his knights;
she could put jam in his coffee and glue in his tea;
she could scramble the channels on his enormous TV.

Anya's eyes were now smarting, and so was her brain,
with all of the scrolling and staring and strain,
and she fell fast asleep with the iPad still on,
and when she awoke the battery had gone.

After breakfast, she secretly put it on charge
And stood it with her books, or those that were large,
and all of that day she was completely distracted
wondering how King Trevelyan might have reacted.

That night, she didn't dare tell her mum yet again
she was going to bed early, so she stayed up 'til ten.
But then she gave a great yawn, kissed her mother goodnight
and went up to bed and turned off the light.

Once under the duvet, she clicked the iPad to 'On'.
The battery was charged and the touch-screen shone,
lighting up the tent she had made with her knees
(she noticed her feet smelt a little bit of cheese!).

She would not be afraid, she'd be determined and strong –
she'd been planning her next move all the day long.
Scrolling through icons, she tapped with her nail
on the app that was labelled 'King Trevelyan's e-mail.'

Then she typed out a message with a trembling heart,
she was contacting the King, she was making a start!
'Dear King,' she began, and then hit the backspace,
he wasn't at all 'dear,' he was just a disgrace.

Instead, she wrote simply 'If you're wondering why
the colours in your palace have gone all awry
I'm writing to tell you the reason is this –
you're a very bad king, the worst that there is.

You must free all the prisoners and lower the taxes
or there'll be more surprises, snafus and banjaxes.'
She worried the King would know who had dared to offend,
but thought of her father, shut her eyes, and pressed 'Send.'

Now she had done it, there was no going back,
and for hour after hour she lay quite awake,
worrying about how angry King Trevelyan would be
when he opened his email with his first cup of tea.

But she thought of her dad in that horrid dark cell
and all of the others in the dungeons as well,
and resolved to use all the power she now had
to torment Trevelyan and drive him quite mad.

The app for 'King's larder' showed a scene of great gluttony,
with two tons of beef and one ton of muttony,
for Trevelyan, it was said, ate more than an elephant
(which would help to explain the size of his belly-front),

Then she noticed a slider she could drag either way –
one end was transparent and the other was grey.
The label to the right said 'Strongest of all'
and the one on the left said 'No taste at all.'

For each of the foods in the King's larder that day,
She soon had the flavour all draining away.
It was nearly morning now, she could hear the first birds
as she tapped on 'King's e-mail' and wrote out the words:

'The people all say you are horrid and incorrigible,
so from now on your food will be horrid and porridgible.
And until you release all the people from jail
every day you'll be getting another e-mail.'

Trevelyan's Torments

Now our story will say goodbye for a while,
to the little girl in her bedroom and travel ten miles
to the palace itself, all brown, green and blue,
to see how things looked from the King's point of view.

In the royal apartments the first thing we find
is a dishevelled Trevelyan nearly out of his mind.
Everything's going wrong, he doesn't know what to do,
his food tastes of nothing and his bed sheets are blue.

His life has become almost totally contrarian,
his dogs that loved hunting have turned vegetarian
and every new day something else goes all wrong
and always there's an email following along

to tell him the reason for the latest calamity
is that he and his soldiers lack all humanity;
he's hated by the people and will very soon find
that things will get worse if he doesn't resign!

Only yesterday morning he'd planned an invasion
of some other country, European or Asian,
he'd trotted out his horses and marshalled his forces
(having eaten a breakfast of six tasteless courses),

but when he had given the stern order to march
and imagined his statue and a triumphal arch,
he found that the trumpets gave out not a peep,
and the whole of his army had fallen asleep.

Not long after that his e-mail went 'ping'
with a message that properly infuriated the King,
and he said that if he ever ... if he ever discovered
who was sending the emails, he'd make sure they suffered.

But the truth was the King was becoming worn down
and beginning to wish he'd never seen a gold crown.
All his pleasures, it seemed, had just turned to dust
and all of his treasures had started to rust.

When he put on some music, he only got screams.
He couldn't get to sleep, and if he slept he had dreams
of the people of Morvan, all wretched and poor,
heading straight for the palace to beat down his door.

His soap wouldn't wash and his towels wouldn't dry,
His dogs wouldn't bark, his hawks wouldn't fly,
His fridge warmed things up and his lollipops melted,
his shoes pinched his feet, his pants came unbelted.

His fingernails were growing an inch every day,
His telescope made everything look further away.
He found that he'd lost seven inches in height,
and his radiators clanked in the middle of the night.

His coffee wouldn't grind, his cup wouldn't sup,
his dog had a kitten, his cat had a pup,
his courtiers forgot how they ought to address him
and his glamorous girlfriend just upped and left him.

His shoes wouldn't shine, his clothes were in tatters,
and his trusted advisers were all mad as hatters.
His money wouldn't be counted, his sight had grown dim,
his channels wouldn't change, someone cancelled his SIM,

His kettle wouldn't boil and his teeth wouldn't brush,
his fires wouldn't light and his loo wouldn't flush.
The rings in his ears had lost all their glitter,
no one 'Liked' him on Facebook, no one followed him on Twitter.

His shower had no power and his bath wouldn't fill,
his custard was lumpy, his wines wouldn't chill,
his toast wouldn't brown and his verbs wouldn't noun,
his ring wouldn't bling and his turn-ups turned down.

Someone cancelled his policies and broke his alliances
and blew all the fuses in his electric appliances.
And day after day he became more distracted –
his oven cooled things down, his pet adder subtracted.

And all of this happened because, quite out of sight,
a little girl was busy in the middle of the night,
rearranging the life of King Trevelyan the Mighty
and driving him mad, all snug in her nightie.

Now none of this was secret, the palace servants all knew,
and they told everybody, insisting it was true.
The people all followed the story on computers
and drove around town all sounding their hooters

at every new calamity that happened at the Palace –
it was better than Game of Thrones, it was better than Dallas.
Every night the whole nation was turning the telly on
for the latest instalment of Carry on Trevelyan.

Everybody it seemed watched the King's downward spiral;
on YouTube the video had overnight gone viral.
Millions logged on, the whole world was agog,
And some of the King's servants had started a blog.

Then finally a time came when the King had had enough
and could no longer be bothered to huff and to puff,
Every day without fail some new disaster befell him
and finally his advisers decided to tell him

he'd better give up, go abroad, abdicate,
and maybe, just maybe, going away might placate
whoever it was who was playing this game,
tormenting his days and driving him insane.

Trevelyan lay on his bed and said 'Do what you please,'
and summoned his jailer and gave him the keys
to the overflowing dungeons saying 'Let them all out,'
and he said it very quietly, too exhausted to shout.

So the jailer announced that on Saturday next
All the prisoners' families could come and collect
their fathers and brothers and daughters and mothers
who'd been kept in the dungeons with so many others.

Anya heard the good news that same afternoon
when her mum picked her up and swung her round the room.
'Guess what?' she said happily, putting her down,
'your dad's being freed and we're going to town

to get him out of prison and bring him back home.
We'll take him some food and a brush and a comb,
now we'll all be together for ever and more,
and Trevelyan has gone, we don't have to be poor!'

Anya laughed and cried too, she was feeling quite heady
as she rushed around helping her mum to get ready
and trying not to show that her joy was still fearful
for often each day she had felt herself tearful

when she remembered the night she'd clicked on the icon
that said 'King's Dungeons' where there was never a light on
but only great darkness and soft moans of despair
from the innocent people held prisoner there.

On the Saturday morning, they set off before seven
(for the distance to town was ten miles or eleven)
and they wanted to be sure to be there by three
when the dungeon was opened and the prisoners set free.

When they arrived in the square there was already a crowd
of relatives impatiently calling out loud
for the jail to be opened; it was ten minutes past three
when the jailer arrived with a great iron key.

Anya bit her lip and hardly dared look
as the great gates opened and the inmates all took
their first steps to freedom, dazzled by the light,
blinking and stumbling, their faces all white.

As the long line of prisoners staggered and straggled
into the town square, all gaunt and bedraggled,
it should have been easy to spot someone so tall,
but of Anya's dad there was no sign at all.

Until there was just one man, standing alone,
he was upright and tall but all skin and bone
as he blinked in the sunlight and gulped the fresh air,
and ran one bony hand through his long straggly hair.

He looked straight at Anya and her mother beside her
and attempted a smile as his arms opened wider.
And underneath all the dirt and the beard
they saw who it was and the crowd around cheered

as they ran to his arms and helped him to stand
and kissed him and hugged him and clung to his hand
all the way to their village, stopping often to rest,
where he slept for two days, they thought it was best.

The Night Visitor

Two months have now passed and, slowly each day,
life in Morvan became better, I'm happy to say.
Anya's dad put on weight and was well on the mend
while Anya was in school and back in the band.

The king was long gone who had made such a mess,
and was last heard of living in a caravan in Skegness.
All the people rejoiced at Trevelyan's going
and wherever he was, they hoped it was snowing.

Anya's mum and dad joined in the popular call
For a meeting of citizens in the town hall,
and it seemed that with no king to make an objection
there was going to be something called a general election.

'What's that?' said Anya, will it come in the post?'
'I'll tell you,' said her mother, 'if you eat up your toast.
It's a way of deciding who'll govern the country
so everything works and no one goes hungry.

'All those who think they'd be good at the job
put their names on a list – Sunil, Maya or Bob –
and then all of the people have to put a big tick
by the name of the one who's their favourite pick.

And the one with most ticks is duly elected
which just means to say he or she's been selected
as the person most people believe would be best
to govern the country and not be a pest.'

Anya listened for a while and thought of Morwena
who went on like this if you didn't restrain her,
about politics and pensions and bothersome things
and general elections and not having kings.

That night just as Anya was falling asleep
there came from the bookshelf ... a little 'beep, beep'.
Standing up on her bed, she took down the screen
which by now, it was true, could have done with a clean.

She rubbed at her eyes but couldn't quite make out
the shifting black figure that was shuffling about
but gradually she saw, in the dark shapes and light,
that Morwena had come visiting in the deep of the night.

'Hi there, Anya sweetheart, I hope you're, like, well,'
said the witch with a smile, 'I know it's past twelve,
but I thought I'd drop in just to see how you were
and also to say, like, 'Well done, my dear?'

'I've been watching it all on my own little screen
and I wanted to tell you what fun it's all been.'
'You know the King's gone?' Anya said in a whisper.
'Of course,' said the witch, 'I heard from my sister'.

‘And I see now, my dear, there’s to be an election
though that's no guarantee of governmental perfection.
But it's better than kings or hereditary royalty
Which might be okay but might be idiotoyalty.

‘Now remember to come visit whenever you have time,
You can toast up some chocolate and, like, help me with rhyme.
But I guess it might be difficult – that’s okay, I’m cool –
you’ll have lots of homework now you’re at school.’

‘Oh, I will come and visit,’ said Anya, too loudly.
‘Not tomorrow,’ said the witch, ‘it's going to be cloudly.’
‘I was wondering,’ said Anya, ‘if it would be okay to tell –
just Mum and Dad – the whole story, as well ... ?’

‘I suppose you can tell them,’ said the witch interrupting,
‘since they are responsible for your bringing-up-ting,
but really my dear I’d very much rather
you didn’t show the iPad to your fother and mather.’

‘Of course,’ promised Anya, all happy and glowing,
she’d hated the idea of her mum and dad not knowing.
‘I’ll come see you soon, can I bring you anything?’
‘No thanks,’ said the witch I’ve, like, got everything.’

The very next morning over brown eggs and toast,
Anya started on the story, though she tried not to boast.
Her mum and dad listened with sceptical expressions
and kept interrupting with annoying grownups’ questions

as she told of her visit to the old witch's cave
and the lines of dark washing and the flowers she gave
to the kindly Morwena who, though a thousand years old,
was a whizz with computers and could programme in code.

Then she told how the tablet had quite done the trick
once she'd learnt how to swipe and to tap and to click
on the icons and sliders that allowed her to change
everything in the King's life and drive him insane.

'She's always been good,' said her dad, 'at making up stories.'
'Magic iPad!' said her Mum, 'you're as bad as the Tories.'
'But it's true, every word,' said Anya, frustrated,
'I wish you'd believe me, I'm quite agitated.'

The Queen's Return

Now the people of Morvan were free of the King,
but they missed the parades and the national bling,
and it seemed that the obvious thing to be done
was to ask Queen Sue-Li to stop being a nun

and return to the palace and be sure to bring Ruff,
for the people had missed his friendly 'ruff-woof.'
So the Queen came back to a popular clamour,
with a diamond tiara, which added some glamour.

To welcome her home a parade had been planned
with a funfair and fireworks and of course a brass band,
and all the Morvanis turned out to greet her
in the square where the Prime Minister waited to meet her.

Among the large crowd that gathered that day,
on a warm afternoon at the back end of May
were all of the members of the family Castagna
And right at the front was – you guessed it – Anya.

A great cheer arose as the Queen's carriage came by,
The Queen smiling and waving, Ruff wagging behind
(The nuns had been kind, but anyone could see
that a dog in a nunnery was barking up the wrong tree).

Then the strangest thing happened amidst all the cheering
for as the Queen's horses and carriage were nearing,
old Ruff left the parade and headed straight up to Anya,
ears pricked and tale wagging, etcetera etcetera,

and bow-bowing before her began licking her hand,
as the parade passed on by, and with it the band.
It was almost as if ... as if each lick was a 'Thank you,'
It was almost as if ... as if somehow Ruff knew!

Warm tears of happiness came to Anya's eyes
As Ruff barked two or three times to say his goodbyes,
then ran after the carriage and tripped up the band
as Anya stared down at her very damp hand.

And now our little story need not be lengthened
except for one detail that ought to be mentioned.
It concerns Anya's mum who decided one morning
To paint Anya's bedroom without any warning.

As she placed all the books in a box on the floor
she came across one that weighed a bit more
and she saw as she lifted it down from the wall
That it didn't have pages ... no pages at all!

As it dropped from her hands, the cover flew open
to reveal a glass screen with a flashing pink slogan:
'To securely log on to Worldwide Witches' Coven –
Enter your password in English or Russian'.

The battery then died and with it the screen,
but just for a moment she thought she had seen
A shadowy figure who froze in a pose,
With a pointed black hat and a very long nose.

The End

Acknowledgements

Many thanks to all who have given help and advice with the preparation of this book including Naomi Smith, Colin Smith, Lesley Adamson, Chris Brazier, Helen Longworth and Charlie Webster.